# Scenes From The Last Journey

# Scenes From The Last Journey

## 14 Points On The Way Of The Cross

Richard P. Zimmerman

NOVO CIVITAS BOOKS AND RESOURCES
Seattle, Washington

SCENES FROM THE LAST JOURNEY
14 Points On The Way Of The Cross

Novo Civitas Books and Resources
Novocivitas.com




Copyright © 2021 by Richard P. Zimmerman

All rights reserved. No part of this book may be reproduced in any form without the written permission of the author, with the exception of brief excerpts for the purpose of review.

PAPERBACK ISBN 9780578868134
EBOOK ISBN 9780578868141

Go to dark Gethsemane,
Ye that feel the tempter's power;
Your Redeemer's conflict see,
Watch with him one bitter hour;
Turn not from his griefs away,
Learn of Jesus Christ to pray.

    Follow to the judgment-hall
    View the Lord of life arraigned;
    O the wormwood and the gall!
    O the pangs his soul sustained!
    Shun not suffering, shame, or loss;
    Learn of him to bear the cross.

        Calvary's mournful mountain climb;
        There, adoring at his feet,
        Mark that miracle of time,
        God's own sacrifice complete:
        "It is finished!" hear him cry;
        Learn of Jesus Christ to die.

*Early hasten to the tomb,*
*Where they laid his breathless clay;*
*All is solitude and gloom;*
*Who hath taken him away?*
*Christ is risen; he meets our eyes;*
*Saviour, teach us so to rise!*

        James Montgomery

# Contents

|   |   |   |
|---|---|---|
|   | Where The Sorrow Began | 1 |
|   | Walk | 7 |
|   | Guidance For How To Use This Book | 13 |
|   | An Opening Prayer | 21 |
| 1 | Jesus Predicts The Betrayal | 25 |
| 2 | Prayer In The Garden | 29 |
| 3 | The Arrest | 35 |
| 4 | Trials | 41 |
| 5 | Peter Denies Knowing Jesus | 47 |
| 6 | Jesus is Scourged And Crowned With Thorns | 51 |
| 7 | Pilate Washes His Hands Jesus Is Condemned To Death | 55 |
| 8 | The Road To Crucifixion | 61 |
| 9 | The Soldiers Crucify Jesus | 65 |

| 10 | Jesus Speaks From The Cross | 69 |
| 11 | Jesus Cries Out | 73 |
| 12 | The Last Breath | 77 |
| 13 | Jesus Is Taken Down From The Cross | 81 |
| 14 | Jesus Is Laid In A Tomb | 85 |
|    | A Closing Prayer | 89 |
|    | Appendix 1: A Word About This Translation | 95 |
|    | Appendix 2: The Traditional 14 Stations Of The Cross | 101 |
|    | In Gratitude | 109 |
|    | Bibliography | 113 |

# Where The Sorrow Began

Sometimes the Gospel writers tell us about who Jesus is by showing what he has done. Sometimes they report his words. Sometimes they throw his character into sharp focus by describing episodes of opposition, and insights arise by seeing what kinds of people were set against him and why. Though the Gospel writers generally leave their own personalities out of their Gospels, each one brings a certain perspective to the story. This is mostly done by choosing to include particular episodes and leaving out others, but sometimes a comment is included as well.

This is true throughout each Gospel. Matthew shows wise men traveling a long way from lands far to the east in response to a star in the night sky. Luke reports the visitations of angels from heaven at important moments of confirmation. Mark unfolds healing stories in staccato fashion, showing the power of Jesus over the forces of death. And John tells us directly from the beginning that Jesus is the eternal Word of God in human form, a revelation of God's glory, and that he is "full of grace and truth."

# Scenes From The Last Journey

*Full of grace and truth.* This phrase is delivered in the beginning of John's Gospel as a promise of what anyone will find who explores the real nature of Jesus. It is as though John is saying, "Read this book and you will find something you have never before encountered: a person who is full of grace and truth."

This is most pointedly true as the story intensifies during the last hours of Jesus's life.

Grace and truth are both challenges. We all think we are in favor of grace and truth but it is not too long before grace and truth become uncomfortable. Many people fight for the truth as they perceive it and for grace for their own failures. But when the truth confronts *them,* or the grace is poured out for an enemy, the story takes a turn. This is what happened to Jesus when he came his own with a message of grace and truth.

The last 24 hours of the life of Jesus tell the story of the forces of evil turning violent against the grace and truth he offered. Since four voices narrate the last 24 hours of his life., and since these four Gospels tell what happened in far greater detail than at any other time of his life, we have a great deal of information about that last day. While spare in details for a long number of preliminary chapters, the Gospels suddenly spring to narrative fullness as all four writers seem eager for us to know everything about how those last 24 hours progressed.

The reason for each unique perspective comes into sharp focus in those final hours of each Gospel narrative. And yet it is not the witness of any single Gospel writer, but the overwhelming message of all four together that truly tells this story.

I have created a blended narrative of all four Gospels so that the story, as told by all four Gospel writers, can be read as one. Once that whole narrative was complete I selected 14 episodes within the story as meditational points along the journey of his final hours. These 14 scenes are presented here as a way of walking with Jesus through his last hours on Good Friday.

The first event of that last day[1] is known as "the last supper." This is the day we remember with communion. Communion means to take into our lives the living presence of Christ—to be with him in the most important sense. So it is heartbreaking and jarring to reflect on how lonely the path was that Jesus walked on Good Friday. To offer himself to his friends at the table in the upper room was a most intimate act.

Hours later in the garden, when the soldiers had him surrounded, all of the fears of the disciples of Jesus came true. Jesus was taken captive. But he secured the release of his disciples by requesting of the soldiers to let them go. In this way he spared them from joining him in death. He asserted to the guards that his companions should be released and not arrested with him. In sparing them he made a lonely path for his last hours. No one else was with him. Grace and truth meant walking a lonely road. He had to walk the road of suffering all by himself.

---

[1] In the Bible's way of counting time, day begins at sunset and proceeds until sunset on the following day. So the last day of the life of Jesus goes from the last supper until the following sunset, just after the body of Jesus is laid in the tomb

But in every moment we have the chance to reverse that loneliness by walking with him. This is most pointedly true on Good Friday. That is a day when we have a chance walk the road to the cross and remember what he suffered so that we might live in freedom and abundance forever.

When we recite the Apostles' Creed we remember that Jesus "suffered under Pontius Pilate, was crucified, dead, and buried;" A similar phrase is in the Nicene Creed. The letters of the New Testament build many of their concepts on the sacrifice of Jesus for us on this day. And while the resurrection is the most central truth of the Bible, the resurrection could not happen without Good Friday. The whole picture of his suffering presents us with the whole sufficiency of his grace. If there is any tendency to question whether such a sacrifice is enough, if there is any lingering doubt of his loving commitment to your best interest, if any shadow of guilt still haunts your days or awakens you in the night, then let this journey with Jesus relieve you. Take this time to let it sink in. Jesus suffered and died so that you could be pardoned from your sins and healed from your wounds. Let this become the application of the grace waiting for all of those who put their trust in Jesus.

Saint Augustine made note of the gain that might come from placing ourselves in these scenes with the disciples and friends of Jesus. Taking note of the reference in Mark 15:40 to the women who were "looking on" when Jesus died, he writes,

> As they were "looking on," so we too gaze on his wounds as he hangs. We see his blood as he dies. We see the price offered by the redeemer, touch the scars of his resurrection. He bows his head, as if to

kiss you. His heart is made bare open, as it were, in love to you. His arms are extended that he may embrace you. His whole body is displayed for your redemption. Ponder how great these things are. Let all this be rightly weighed in your mind: as he was once fixed to the cross in every part of his body for you, so he may now be fixed in every part of your soul.[2]

We live in a world that has seen the defeat of death through the resurrection of Jesus, and we celebrate that victory every Easter and in every moment. So this observance of Good Friday is a reflection back on a world of suffering that has been defeated. And yet we still live in a world staggering under the weight of cruelty and death. These 14 scenes from Good Friday testify to God's willingness to be crushed under that weight–crushed, but not defeated. From a true contemplation of the depth of this love will spring a transformation, as St. Augustine says, "fixed in every part of your soul."

## A Finished Work

What Jesus did on his last day on earth accomplished something that is forever finished. (See Hebrews 10:11-14) Be careful to cling to that truth as you walk this path. It is tempting to erase the finality of Jesus's work by believing that our observance of the importance of this day somehow adds to or completes the work that Jesus has done. Instead, think of this meditation as a way of applying his completed work to your experience of his grace.

---

[2] St. Augustine, *On Virginity*, quoted from *Ancient Christian Commentary on Scripture*, New Testament II, Mark, 235.

## Scenes From The Last Journey

◀   ◀   ◀

If this is a darker and deeper journey than you normally take on Good Friday, let me urge one last thing before we leave this introduction. Let Easter be lighter, happier, richer, and more care-free than ever before. If you have chosen to linger on the lonely road of Good Friday, make every effort to leave behind every sin and every sorrow when you celebrate the resurrection. Rejoice with all your heart.

# Walk

I first visited Jerusalem when I was 16 years old. The reality of walking the same streets that Jesus walked had a profound impact on my young imagination. Among the many places where Jesus surely walked is the road he traveled following his trial. This route, known as the *Via Dolorosa* (Way of Sorrows), is prominently marked with 14 stations. These stations mark stopping–points along the road that Jesus walked when he took his last steps in his earthly life. These stations commemorate 14 particular events when Jesus traveled from condemnation, to the cross, to the tomb.

As I walked those streets I considered and critiqued my own faith in the resurrected Jesus who lives today, and I became deeply aware of how far short my commitment to him fell. Back home, at my high school, my constant hope was that no one would find out I was a Christian. I didn't want to be labeled as "one of those." I didn't want to try to explain my faith. I didn't want to make any life choices that marked me as different from my friends at school. In short, I wanted all of the benefits of eternal life promised to me by my church without any of the suffering associated with walking in the footsteps of Jesus.

## Scenes From The Last Journey

In retrospect, I can see how my adolescent intellectual and emotional development had come to a ripe moment that summer. I was ready to recognize the childishness of my faith. That readiness converged with the profound setting—the sights and sounds of Jerusalem. While I was on that trip I only wondered, only questioned, only inwardly shrank back in shame at my own cowardice. But when I left Israel in early August to return home I brought with me the questions and self-critiques. And in the remaining weeks of the summer that experience resolved into a new commitment. I was transported from the one kind of faith, a childish and selfish faith, into a new way of living. Prior to walking those streets my attitude, for the most part, implied that I believed Jesus was lucky to have gotten anything out of me. The profound challenge of the way of the cross left me certain I did not deserve anything from him, and grateful that he has chosen to give me everything.

◀ ◀ ◀

People have walked the road of Jesus's suffering every Good Friday for many hundreds of years. And all around the world people came to realize that a meditational journey can be created anywhere. Fourteen stopping points mark specific events in that one day of the life of Christ. These are known as

*Walk*

the *14 Stations of the Cross*. They mark events from when Jesus was condemned to death until he was laid in the tomb. Some of these events traditionally included are not narrated in our Gospels, but instead come from later traditions associated with the events of Good Friday.

As I describe this you may have images in your mind of wailing martyrs flagellating themselves as they march along on Good Friday. No doubt things like that may occur. But that is not necessarily the essence of this spiritual practice. Rather than inflicting the pain of that last journey on ourselves, we can instead take this as a reminder that Jesus suffered to liberate us from the oppression of our guilt—not to make us inflict payment on ourselves for our transgressions.

As I considered the potential value of this journey with Jesus, it seemed to me that though the practice of physically reliving these hours in his life is a good thing, a few adjustments could make this more effective for those who are not walking that road in Jerusalem but are instead remembering these events from far away in their own setting. The ordeal began for Jesus with the tremendous sorrow of betrayal. Jesus shared with his disciples the news that one of them was going to break the trust of their friendship. When Jesus announced this to them as they were seated around the table of his last meal, events were set in motion that would shortly lead to his death. So the stations I have outlined begin with the announcement of the betrayal. That is where the sorrow began.

Through my study of the scriptures I have created a set of 14 stations similar to the stations in Jerusalem. The 14 events recounted in this book come directly from the pages of the four Gospels. These are not identical with the traditional 14 stations. Instead, these 14 points along the last journey of Jesus have been selected to reflect the Biblical accounts from the betrayal and arrest until Jesus is laid in the tomb.

This tells the story from beginning to end, but it doesn't tell the whole story. These 14 scenes have been selected out of the entire narrative. For a complete account of everything reported by the four Gospels during those 24 hours, see my book, *Down The Last Road: The Last Day of the Earthly Life of Jesus*.

I have brought together an original translation of all four Gospels to create this narrative of the last hours. I could have tracked all of the various scripture references and listed the biblical references so that you could flip back and forth between the gospel accounts and read for yourself, from your own Bible, the narrative of these events as each of the 4 witnesses report them. But the concentration needed to look up these verses would take your mind away from the narrative of the events themselves. You would spend a great deal of time flipping pages. Alternatively, you could simply pick one of the Gospels and read the passages that narrate these events from that one Gospel. While it is undoubtedly of great value to read each individual Gospel account regarding this day, Good Friday is a time for reflection on the whole series of events, from when Jesus was arrested until his body was laid in the tomb. We have four Gospels for a reason. We need all of them to get the complete story. Taking note of chapter and verse and marking the particular details of each gospel is an important line of study, but there is also value in an uninterrupted concentration on the most important points in the narrative without thinking at all about the Gospel writers themselves. So I created this blended translation to assist you in a meditational reading of all four Gospels at once. For a detailed description of how this blended translation was created, see Appendix 1.

I hope you will lose yourself in the flow and be transported in your imagination to the very scenes of the suffering of Jesus. This is not out of some morbid fascination with the cruelty of humanity. Rather, this meditational practice is intended to unfurl the full extent of the love Jesus has for you.

## *Physical Movement As Part Of This Reading*

I highly recommend finding some way of incorporating walking from place to place as part of this spiritual practice. It is good to slowly read through each of these 14 moments. But is even better to walk a pathway and pause 14 times to read the Bible passages narrating each event, and then to linger and reflect on what you have read before walking to the next station. This rhythm of reading, pausing, walking, has a way of involving more than just the mind. Let the story penetrate deeper than the mind alone. Consider how the actual movement through time and space can be an immersive experience of prayer. So frequently we rush through the reading of the Bible, perhaps spending too much time within a surface impression of what took place rather than deeply considering the significance of what we are reading. The time it takes to walk from one station to the next becomes a time for contemplating what the witnesses to these events are really telling us about what happened.

In search of a more spiritual life, Christians often neglect or disregard the body. But some spiritual practices have a greater impact on the spirit when they are integrated with actions of the body. More than simply reading about Jesus walking through the streets of Jerusalem carrying a crossbeam on his shoulders, walk for a time with the gospel narrative of those moments fresh in your mind and the experience will have a greater impact on your whole being. What would it be like to walk from the garden of Gethsemane, bound and in custody, knowing that your capture was entirely arranged by one of your chosen followers? That agony of betrayal is nearly beyond my imagination. Taking the time to meditate, ponder, and actually walk from one place to another is the best way I know to receive the grace of knowing that Jesus forgives betrayers like me and you.

# Guidance For How To Use This Book

Time and creativity will most likely guide you to the best use of this book. I am a firm believer in the value of locally designed worship and learning events. And yet it is often helpful to have someone to talk with, someone who has used the resource before, as a conversation partner in the planning stages. So think of this next section as a conversation with me as I share what has worked best in my churches in the past.

### Setting Up Actual Stations

It can be very helpful when individuals or churches set up actual physical stations along a trail and offer a book to guide each person or group to direct them to read the Bible passages associated with each event. One congregation I served had a grove of trees with a pathway through it. We made 14 large posters with the numbers of each station on each one, with a brief caption of what took place at that station. Then we found objects to represent the main action of each station and we set those objects underneath each of the numbers. So, for example, at Station 7, where Pilate condemns Jesus to death and then washes his hands, we placed a large bowl filled with water and a towel was set beside it. Setting up the stations can be simple or more involved, depending on what you have time to do. The artistic and expressive people in your congregation may be willing to take on the project and add some visual references to each station.

## *Some Planning Will Help*

So many great opportunities for Christian discipleship are built into the calendar of the church. In preparation for Lent and Holy Week, some comprehensive planning should be undertaken to craft experiences for people to engage with the Gospel accounts of those events that stand at the core of our faith. Plans for Good Friday should fit in with the big picture of what you have planned on Palm Sunday, Maundy Thursday, and Easter. Spend a little time brainstorming about where the pathway for the 14 stations may be placed in your community. Then invest some effort in creating a physical pathway that will match the stations in this book. The distances do not need to be great. It could be as simple as 14 posters attached to the walls of the fellowship hall of your church. But keep in mind that if multiple groups are traveling through the stations at the same time, and if they are reading out loud, and if the stations are within earshot of one another, the multiple voices can be distracting.

## Guidance For How To Use This Book

Consider asking someone or some group to prepare the stations. The act of making some visual representation for each episode can be a rewarding experience of spiritual growth. You could choose an artist in the community to make sketches of each scene. You could have the children in Sunday School draw the events described, or go on a scavenger hunt to find physical objects that remind them of each scene. You could choose 14 families and ask them each to decorate one station in a way that will provide a visual supplement to the reading.

### *Individuals Or Groups Can Go Through The Stations*

Some people will want to walk through the stations and read the passages for themselves. Others will be better off if they travel through with a group and listen as the passages are read out loud. The individuals in each group may take turns reading the passages at each station. Groups might consist of families, home Bible study groups, Sunday School classes, or youth groups. Suggest to your leaders that they may want to plan a time for walking the path together with their groups.

### *A Designated Reader At Each Station*

A different approach would be to recruit 14 readers and distribute them at the stations. When an individual or group approaches the station the reader would then read the text. The point of this would be to make it so that the participants hear the scriptures at every point without distraction, and without the need for concentrating on the words. An auditory experience is more powerful for many people, while others are more likely to get the most out of a participatory experience where they are involved in the process of reading.

Consider also that you are in a better position to invite the general public to participate if you use designated readers at each station. Those who are not familiar with the story of the suffering of Jesus may be more able to take it in if they are only asked to move from station to station and listen as the passages are being read.

If you place readers at the stations a general time frame must be established and announced or you would have to keep the readers in place all day. If people are given their own copies of this book they may be invited to make their way through the stations at any time all day.

## *Flexibility May Be Crucial*

If rain is in the forecast, maybe the "trail" will need to be moved indoors.[3] It won't be like walking through the streets of Jerusalem, but still, moving from place to place and reading the passages for each station will make for an experience of spiritual growth. Consider the unique layout of your church building and try to imagine how this walk may be constructed within it. If physical limitations make it difficult to actually establish a trail, participants may use a booklet for a guide for meditation at home on Good Friday. Though they won't walk around to actual stations, they can travel in their minds to experience the love of Jesus in his sacrifice for the world.

Over the years I have found that when events interrupt my plans the outcome is often much better than my original

---

[3] One year, in rainy Oregon, we laminated the posters that marked the stations, but kept the stations outside. In the end we had differing opinions on whether that was a good decision as we evaluated the soggy outcome.

vision. When an idea gets thwarted, that only leaves an opportunity for something better to emerge.

## *Incorporated Into Worship*

Having spent all of this time advocating for some sort of a trail with 14 stations, I must also say that these readings might well form the narrative for a brief Good Friday service of worship. A few songs might be added, and a brief message could be inserted at many different points along the way, depending on the topic of the sermon. Some churches have a noon-time Good Friday service and the reading of these passages could easily be done while still leaving people time to get back to work on their lunch hour. Or a service on the evening of Good Friday might allow time for more prayer or other worship elements.

While it is important for each individual to consider the call to follow Jesus on the way of the cross, don't underestimate the value of having your congregation unite around this central event of our faith.

## *Remember Those Who Are Homebound*

This book can easily be used to serve those who have a hard time getting out of their homes for worship. Teams of people could visit those who are homebound and read the passages, allowing time for reflection between each station. Even simply mailing copies of this book to the homebound members of your congregation may be an encouraging step.

## *Family Use*

In some ways this story may be too much for children, especially in its raw and complete form. And yet the impact of the death of Jesus is most powerful because Jesus exposed the evil in this world in the truest sense. Is it really possible that Jesus could be born into the world, could lead a completely sinless life, could teach and heal and gather people into a new community, could exhort everyone to follow God's ways wholeheartedly, and the result would be that we would kill him for it? That is the essence of this story. It is harsh and frightening. Parents need to decide how to introduce children to the raw reality of this story with appropriate timing, or else it could become a bad experience.

Yet at some point, perhaps when the children are in the teen years, parents may decide to read this story as a family to mark the significance of Good Friday. In our home, the time after dinner was often the best time for family worship experiences.

If you choose to do this, be sure and think rather carefully about the impact of this story on the outlook and mood of everyone who participates. Friday night is often a social night, so it may be disconcerting to have dinner, read this narrative, and then go off to some Friday evening entertainment as though nothing significant happened. You will want to plan for a way to process the feelings that might arise out of the narrative. Let family members share what meant the most to them, as well as what parts were troubling. The gloom of this story may be thick, and some of the power of it might linger for a time in the hopelessness that we experience as our social structures can't fix the lurking violence and sin in the world. After all of these years the church is still too much like

## Guidance For How To Use This Book

Judas the betrayer and Peter the denier. And yet leave time for anticipating the coming reality of the hope alive to us at Easter. *Good Friday is not the last word.* Be sure everyone leaves the experience looking forward to the eternal life won for us in the resurrection of Jesus, rather than walking away filled with the dread inherent in the mocking trials, the lash, and the wounds of nails in hands and feet.

The purpose of the 14 Stations journey is to help people make a kind of pilgrimage to the main scenes of Christ's suffering and death. While the suffering and death of Jesus on this day forms part of the most foundational event for our faith, actual observance of Good Friday can easily be neglected. Don't let that happen. Walk with Jesus through this dark valley so that you may enter fully into the joy of his resurrection on Easter.

# An Opening Prayer

# *Opening Prayer*

Jesus our friend, you washed the feet of your disciples when you knew the suffering of this day lay ahead for you. Your mercy is beyond our comprehension and your love is more durable than our weakness.

Forgive us for having trampled on your forgiveness by the indifference of our daily lives. We do not deserve the endless stream of love that constantly pours forth from your cross. We do now truly repent of our complacency and we turn to you again. Help us once again to enter into the secure peace of your death defying love.

Lord, as we draw near to the way of your suffering and death we begin to hear the jeering crowds. We see the agony on your face. We feel the desperation of your friends as they watched you being taken away. Help us to see that your sorrow was for our lost lives. You found us worth saving.

Amen.

# Jesus Predicts The Betrayal

Matthew 26:21-24, Mark 14:18-21,
Luke 22:21-23, & John 13:21-30

# Jesus Predicts The Betrayal

Jesus and his disciples were at the table, eating. Jesus was deeply troubled in spirit and he solemnly declared, "I tell you truly, one of you is going to betray me."

His disciples looked around at each another, completely uncertain as to which of them he meant. They were very sad and began to say to him one after another, "Surely not I, Lord?"

One disciple, one whom Jesus loved, was reclining next to him. Simon Peter motioned to that disciple and said, "Ask him who he means."

So the disciple leaned back toward Jesus and asked, "Lord, who?"

Jesus answered, "The one who has dipped his hand into the bowl with me will betray me. The Son of Man will die just as it is written. But such misery will fall upon that man who betrays the Son of Man! It would be better if he had never been born. I will dip bread in a bowl and give it to the one who will betray me."

Then he dipped the bread and gave it to Judas Iscariot, son of Simon. As soon as Judas took the bread, Satan entered into him.

"Hurry and do what you are about to do," Jesus told him, but no one else at the table understood why Jesus said this. Since Judas was in charge of the money, some thought Jesus was telling him to buy things necessary for the festival or to give a gift to the poor. As soon as Judas received the bread he went out into the night.

# Prayer In The Garden

Matthew 26:36-46, Mark 14:32-42, Luke 22:39-46, & John 18:1

## Prayer In The Garden

Jesus said, "Get up, we're going away from this place now."

When they had sung a hymn, Jesus went out as usual to the Mount of Olives, and his disciples came with him. On the other side there was a garden called Gethsemane on the Mount of Olives, and he and his disciples went into it. And Jesus said to them, "Sit here and pray that you won't come under temptation, while I go over there and pray."

He took Peter and the two sons of Zebedee, James and John, along with him, and he began to grieve and to be deeply distressed. Then he said to them, "My soul is overwhelmed with sorrow to the point of death. Stay here and keep watch with me."

Going about a stone's throw away, he fell with his face to the ground and asked that, if possible, this hour might pass him by. "Abba, Father, you can do everything. May this cup be taken from me. Yet not as I want, but as you will."

An angel from heaven then appeared to him, strengthening him. He continued praying even more earnestly. And drops of his sweat fell to the ground like drops of blood.

He got up from prayer, returned to his disciples and found them sleeping, exhausted by their grief. "Why are you sleeping? Could all of you not keep watch with me for one hour?" he asked Peter. "Get up! Watch, and pray so that you won't come under temptation. The spirit is certainly willing but the body is weak."

Going away a second time he again prayed, "My Father, if this cup cannot be taken away unless I drink it, let your will be done."

Again he found them sleeping when he returned because their eyes were heavy. So leaving them, he went away once more and prayed a third time, the same as before.

*Prayer In The Garden*

He then came to the disciples and said to them, "Sleep now and rest. The hour is now arriving for the Son of Man to be betrayed into the hands of sinners. Look! Get up. Let's go! Here comes my betrayer!"

# The Arrest

Matthew 26:52-54, Mark 14:43-52,
Luke 22:47-53, & John 18:2-12

# The Arrest

Now the one betraying him, that is Judas, also knew this place, because Jesus often gathered with his disciples there. So Judas approached leading a band of soldiers and some officials from the chief priests and the Pharisees with lamps, lanterns, and armed with swords and clubs.

The one betraying him had set up a signal: "Whoever I kiss is the one; apprehend him and take him away securely."

Right away he came up to Jesus, Judas said, "Rabbi!" to kiss him.

But Jesus said, "Judas, would you use a kiss to betray the Son of Man?"

Knowing all that was going to happen to him, Jesus asked them, "Who do you want?"

They answered him, "Jesus the Nazarene."

Jesus said to them, "I am."

Now Judas the betrayer stood right there with them. When Jesus said, "I am," they pulled back and fell on the ground.

He asked them again, "Who do you want?"

And they answered, "Jesus the Nazarene."

Jesus answered, "I said to you, 'I am.' So since you are looking for me, allow these others to go."

These words he had spoken were fulfilled in this: "I lost none of those you gave me."

The men laid hands on Jesus and seized him.

Simon Peter had a sword. He drew it and struck the slave of the high priest, and cut off his right ear. The name of the slave was Malchus.

Jesus told Peter, "Put your sword into its sheath! Father has given me this cup. Shall I not drink it? All who draw a sword will die by a sword. Or do you think I don't have the power to ask my Father to provide me at once with more than twelve legions of angels? But then how would the Scriptures be fulfilled that say it must be this way?"

And touching the ear, he cured him.

## The Arrest

Then the detachment of soldiers with its commander and the Jewish officials bound Jesus.

And Jesus said, "As if I am a robber you have come out with swords and clubs to arrest me? I was with you daily in the temple courts teaching, and you did not arrest me. But this is how the Scriptures are fulfilled. This is your hour and the authority of darkness."

Then everyone left him and ran away. Now there was this young man following Jesus, and he was wearing nothing but a linen garment. And they took hold of him, but he left his garment behind and ran away naked.

# Trials

Matthew 26:57-27:26, Mark 14:53-15:15,
Luke 22:54-23:25, & John 18:13-19:16

# Trials

At dawn those who had arrested Jesus took him before Caiaphas the high priest; and all the chief priests, the elders and the teachers of the law had assembled.

Now the chief priests and the whole Sanhedrin were looking for false evidence against Jesus so that they could put him to death. But they did not find any. Though many false witnesses came forward, their statements did not agree. Eventually two came forward and said, "We heard him say, 'I am able to destroy the temple of God made with human hands and build a temple not made with hands over the course of three days.'"

Yet even then their stories did not match one another.

Then the high priest arose and said to Jesus, "Don't you have an answer to the accusations that these men are bringing against you?"

But Jesus stayed silent and gave no answer.

# Scenes From The Last Journey

Again the high priest asked him, "I place you under oath by the living God. Tell us. Are you the Messiah, the Son of the Blessed One?"

Jesus said, "I am. If I tell you, you do not believe me, and if I were to ask you a question, you would never answer. But I declare to all of you, from now on you will see the Son of Man sitting at the right hand of the Mighty One and coming on the clouds of heaven."

Then the high priest tore his clothes and said, "Now you have heard blasphemy! What is your decision?"

"He deserves death," they answered.

Then those who were holding him spit in his face. They blindfolded him and struck him with their fists, and said, "Prophesy for us, Christ! Who is it that hit you?"

And the guards took him and beat him. And they hurled many other insults at him.

### *Jesus Is Turned Over To Pilate*

Then all of the chief priests and the elders of the people bound Jesus and they took him from Caiaphas to the *Praetorium*, the palace of the Roman governor. It was early morning, and to avoid ritual uncleanness they did not enter the *Praetorium*, because they wanted to be able to eat the Passover meal.

### *Pilate Asks What Charges Are Laid Against Jesus*

Pilate came outside to the whole gathering and asked, "What accusations are you bringing against this man?"

## Trials

They were beginning to accuse him, saying, "We discovered this man corrupting our people. He forbids payment of taxes to Caesar and says he is Christ, a king. If he were not doing bad things, we would not have brought him to you."
So Pilate said, "Take him yourselves and judge him according to your own law."

The Jews answered him, "But we are not authorized to kill anyone."

This answer was to fulfill what Jesus had spoken about the kind of death he would die.

### Pilate Asks Jesus, "Are You A King?"

So Pilate went back inside the *Praetorium*, summoned Jesus and said, "Are you the king of the Judeans?"

"You have said so," answered Jesus.

But to the accusations by the chief priests and the elders, he gave no response. Then Pilate asked him, "Don't you hear the many witnesses against you? Aren't you going to answer? Listen to how many accusations there are!"

But Jesus said nothing in response, and Pilate was astonished.

# Peter Denies Knowing Jesus

Matthew 26:69-75, Mark 14:66-72,
Luke 22:55-62, & John 18:17-18, 25-27

# Peter Denies Knowing Jesus

It was cold, and the servants and officials stood around a fire they had kindled to keep warm. Peter also was standing with them, warming himself. When the servant woman saw Peter warming himself, she looked closely at him. "You aren't one of the disciples of that Nazarene, Jesus, are you?" she asked Peter.

He denied it, saying, "I don't know him, woman."

*Peter Denies Knowing Jesus A Second Time*
Simon Peter was still standing by the fire warming himself. When the servant woman saw him there, she said again to those standing around, "This is one of them."

So they asked him, "You are with Jesus the Galilean too, aren't you?"

He denied it, saying, "I am not."

*Peter Denies Knowing Jesus A Third Time*
But one of the servants of the high priest, a relative of the man whose ear Peter had cut off, said, "Didn't I see you in the garden with him?"

Again Peter denied it, "I swear, I don't know who you're talking about," and he went out into the entryway.

At that moment a rooster began to crow. Immediately the rooster crowed a second time. Then Peter remembered what Jesus had told him: "Before the rooster crows twice you will deny you know me three times."

Then he was overcome with bitter weeping.

# Jesus Is Scourged And Crowned With Thorns

Matthew 27:28-31, Mark 15:16-20,
Luke 23:11, & John 19:1-3

# Jesus Is Scourged And Crowned With Thorns

So Pilate took Jesus and had him lashed with a whip. The guards then led Jesus into an interior courtyard of the *Praetorium* and called together the entire troop of soldiers. They stripped his clothes off of him and placed a purple robe around his shoulders. They braided a crown of thorns and placed it on his head and put a staff in his right hand. Falling on their knees, they began to mock-praise him with, "Hail, king of the Jews!"

They spit on him, and took the staff and beat him on the head. They slapped him.

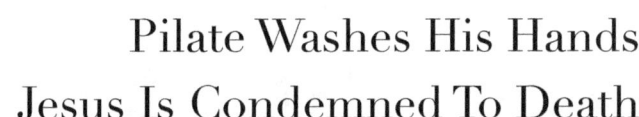

# Pilate Washes His Hands
# Jesus Is Condemned To Death

Matthew 27:15-23, Mark 15:6-14,
Luke 23:17-23, & John 18:39-40; 19:4-15

# Pilate Washes His Hands
# Jesus Is Condemned To Death

Now at the festival it was the governor's custom to release a prisoner chosen by the crowd. At that time they were holding a well-known prisoner named Barabbas. Pilate said to them, "You have a custom that I release for you one prisoner at the time of Passover. Do you want me to release 'the king of the Jews'? Do you want me to release Barabbas, or do you want me to release Jesus who is called the Messiah?" Because he knew it was out of envy that they had delivered Jesus to him.

They shouted back, "No! Give us Barabbas!"

Now Barabbas was a robber. But the chief priests and the elders persuaded the crowd to ask for Barabbas and to have Jesus put to death.

Pilate asked, "Then what will I do with Jesus who is called Christ?"

They all answered, "Crucify him!"

"For what? What evil has he done?" asked Pilate.

But the crowd shouted all the more, "Crucify him!"

Pilate saw that he wasn't getting anywhere, but that instead a riot was beginning. He took water and washed his hands in front of the crowd and said, "I am innocent of this man's blood. See how this is your doing!"

The whole crowd answered, "His blood be upon us and upon our children!"

Then Pilate released Barabbas.

Pilate came out again and said to the crowd, "Listen! I am bringing him outside to you so that you will know that I found no substantial charges against him."

Jesus came outside wearing the thorn crown and the purple robe, and Pilate said, "Here is the man!"

When the chief priests and their attendants saw him, they shouted, "Crucify! Crucify!"

## Pilate Washes His Hands
### Jesus Is Condemned To Death

But Pilate said to them, "Take him and crucify him yourselves. But as for me, I have found no substantial charge against him."

But the Judeans insisted, "We have a law, and according to that law he deserves death, because he claimed he was the Son of God."

So when Pilate heard these words, he grew even more afraid. He went inside the Praetorium again and asked Jesus, "Where do you come from?"

But Jesus didn't give him an answer. So Pilate said, "Do you refuse to speak even to me? Do you not understand? I have authority to set you free and I have authority to crucify you."

Jesus answered, "You would not have power over me at all if it were not given to you from above. So the one who handed me over to you has greater sin than you."

At this, Pilate searched for a way to set Jesus free, but the Judeans called out, "If you release this man you are not a friend of Caesar. Anyone who makes himself out to be a king speaks against Caesar."

So then, when Pilate heard these words, he brought Jesus out and sat down in the tribunal seat at the place known as the Stone Pavement but in Aramaic is called *Gabbatha*. Now it was about the sixth hour on the day of preparation for the Passover. "Here is your king," Pilate said to the Judeans.

But they called out, "Take him! Take him! Crucify him!"

"Your king? Crucify your king?" Pilate asked.

The chief priests answered, "We have no king but Caesar."

So Pilate handed Jesus over to be crucified.

# The Road To Crucifixion

Matthew 27:32, Mark 15:20-21,
Luke 23:26-32, & John 19:17

# The Road To Crucifixion

So the soldiers took Jesus. After they had mocked him, they stripped off the purple robe and put his own clothes back on him. Carrying the cross himself, he went out toward the place of the Skull, which is called Golgotha in Aramaic.

As they went out of the city gate they met a man from Cyrene, named Simon, who was passing by on his way in from the country. Simon was the father of Alexander and Rufus. They put the cross on him and forced him to carry it behind Jesus.

Two others, who were criminals, were being led to be crucified with him.

Now following him there was a large number of people, including women who loudly mourned and wailed for him. But Jesus turned and said to them, "Daughters of

Jerusalem, do not weep for me, but weep for yourselves and for your children, because certainly the days are coming when it will be said,

> 'Childless women are the ones who are blessed;
> the wombs that did not give birth
> and the breasts that never nursed!'

Then

> " 'they will begin to say to the mountains, "Fall on us!"
> and to the hills, "Cover us!"'"

Because if they do these things when the sap is in the tree, what will happen when it is dry?"

# The Soldiers Crucify Jesus

Matthew 27:33-35, Mark 15:22-27,
Luke 23:38, & John 19:17-24

# The Soldiers Crucify Jesus

They brought Jesus to the place called Golgotha, which means "The Place of the Skull." They offered Jesus wine to drink, mixed with something bitter. And he tasted it but he did not drink it.

There they crucified him.

When they had nailed him to the cross they took his clothes and divided them into four shares, one for each of them, with the tunic held out. They distributed his clothes among themselves by chance, casting lots to determine what each one would get. The tunic was woven in one piece from top to bottom, without seams. "Let's not tear it," they said to themselves. "Let's cast a lot for whose it will be."

## Scenes From The Last Journey

This happened in order to fulfill the scripture:
> "They divided my garments among them
> and cast lots for my clothing."

Then they sat down and they kept watch over him. It was the third hour when they crucified him.

*A Written Sign Of The Charges Is Placed Over His Head*

Pilate had a notice prepared and fastened to the cross above his head with the written charge against him. And the notice of the charge read: Jesus of Nazareth, the king of the Judeans. Many Judeans read this sign because the place where Jesus was crucified was near the city, and it was written in Aramaic, Latin and Greek. That led to a protest by the Judean chief priests. They said to Pilate, "Do not write 'The King of the Jews.' But instead write that this man claimed to be king of the Jews."

"What I have written is written," Pilate answered.

# Jesus Speaks From The Cross

Matthew 27:38, Mark 15:27-28, 32 b.,
Luke 23:34 a., 23:39-43, & John 19:18, 19:25-27,

# Jesus Speaks From The Cross

And Jesus said, "Father, forgive them, for they don't know what they are doing."

Near the cross of Jesus stood his mother, his mother's sister, Mary the wife of Clopas, and Mary Magdalene. So when Jesus saw his mother standing nearby and one disciple whom he loved next to her, he said to his mother, "Woman, here is your son." Then to the disciple, "Here is your mother."

From that very hour this disciple took her into his home.

And with him they crucified two robbers, one on his right and one on his left, with Jesus in between.

Then one of the criminals hanging there jeered at him: "You're the Messiah, aren't you? Save yourself and us!"

But the other criminal answered him with a reprimand. "Don't you fear God, since you received the same sentence? It is right for us to be punished, because we are getting back what our actions deserve. But this man did nothing wrong."

Then he said, "Jesus, remember me when you come into your kingdom."

And Jesus told him, "I promise you, today you will be with me in paradise."

# Jesus Cries Out

Matthew 27:46-49, Mark 15:34-36,
& John 19:28-29

# Jesus Cries Out

Then at about three in the afternoon, Jesus cried out in a loud voice, "Eloi, Eloi, l'ma sabachthani?" See Psalm 22:1

That means, "My God, my God, why have you forsaken me?"

Upon hearing this, some of those standing nearby said, "Listen, this man is calling Elijah."

Someone ran and got a sponge. He filled it with bitter wine, put it on a pole, and offered it to Jesus to drink. But the rest said, "Wait. Leave him alone. Let's see if Elijah comes to save him."

After this, Jesus, when he knew that everything had now been completed, in order to fulfill the Scripture, said, "I thirst."

## Scenes From The Last Journey

A container full of bitter wine lay there, so they took a soaked sponge of the bitter wine wrapped around a bunch hyssop stalks, and brought it to his mouth.

# The Last Breath

Matthew 27:50, Mark 15:37-38,
Luke 23:46, & John 19:30

# The Last Breath

When he had taken the bitter wine, Jesus said, "It is completed."

And Jesus called with a loud voice, "Father, into your hands I entrust my spirit." See Psalm 31:5

With that, he bowed his head and gave up his spirit and he breathed his last.

# Jesus Is Taken Down From The Cross

Matthew 27:57-58, Mark 15:42-45,
Luke 23:50-52, & John 19:31-35, 38-39

# Jesus Is Taken Down From The Cross

Now the Judean leaders did not want the bodies left on the crosses during the Sabbath. Since it was the day of Preparation for the next day, especially because this was to be a special Sabbath, they asked Pilate to have the legs of the crucified men broken and their bodies taken down. So the soldiers came and broke the legs of the first one, and then those of the other who had been crucified with Jesus.

But they found Jesus already dead when they came to him so they did not break his legs. But one of the soldiers pierced his side with a spear and a flow of blood and water came out right away. The one who saw these things has given witness, and his testimony is true. And concerning these things he knows that he speaks the truth, so you too may believe.

    As evening approached, there came a rich man from Arimathea, named Joseph. He went boldly to Pilate and made a request for permission to remove body of Jesus. Joseph was a disciple of Jesus, but secretly because he was afraid of the Judean leaders. Joseph was a member of the Council of some stature, who was waiting with hope for the kingdom of God. He was a good and just man, who had not given his consent to the determination or action of the Council.

    Pilate wondered if Jesus was already dead. He called the centurion and questioned him as to whether Jesus had already died. And when he learned from the centurion that Jesus was dead, Pilate gave the order for the body to be released to Joseph. So he came and removed the body. And Nicodemus came also, the one who had first visited Jesus at night. He brought a mixture of myrrh and aloes weighing around seventy-five pounds.

# Jesus Is Laid In A Tomb

Matthew 27:60-61, Mark 15:46 b.-47, Luke 23:53 b.-56, & John 19:41-42

# 14

## Jesus Is Laid In A Tomb

Now there was a garden at the place where Jesus was crucified. And in the garden was a new tomb in which no body had ever been laid. Since the tomb was nearby, and because it was the Jewish day of Preparation, Joseph placed Jesus in his own new tomb that he had cut out of the rock.

Now the women who followed Jesus from Galilee came along following Joseph. They saw the tomb and how his body was placed into it. Joseph rolled a great stone in front of the door to the tomb and went away. Mary Magdalene and Mary the mother of Joseph were sitting there opposite the tomb and saw where his body was laid. Then they returned to where they were staying and prepared aromatic spices and myrrh. And they observed the Sabbath by resting, obeying the commandment.

# A Closing Prayer

# Closing Prayer

We pray to you, heavenly Father, who sent your Son from your side for the sake of your great love for us.

We pray to you, Jesus, who despised the shame of the cross for the sake of our salvation.

We pray to you, Holy Spirit, who makes this saving love known to us.

How great is your love, that you would endure the sorrow of this day for your glory and for our salvation. May we leave this road with a deeper love for you in our hearts. May we look upon all people as your family for whom you were willingly betrayed.

The Father sent Jesus into the world not to condemn the world, but that the world through him might be saved.

Let this day of violence be an end of violence. We look toward the day when you will wipe away every tear and suffering shall be no more.

AMEN.

When I survey
the wondrous cross
On which the Prince
of glory died,
My richest gain
I count but loss,
And pour contempt
on all my pride.

Forbid it, Lord, that I should boast, Save in the death of Christ, my
God; All the vain things that charm me most, I sacrifice them to his blood.

See, from his head,
his hands, his feet,
Sorrow and love
flow mingled down;
Did e'er such love
and sorrow meet,
Or thorns compose
so rich a crown?

Were the whole realm
of nature mine,
That were a present
far too small;
Love so amazing, so divine,
Demands my soul, my life, my all.

Isaac Watts

# Appendix 1

## *A Word About This Translation*
### *And My Method In Creating This Blended Text*

    This project began with my intention to create a blended translation of the narratives in the Gospels of Matthew, Mark, Luke and John that was neither critical nor reconstructive. In this way my blended translation is somewhat different from other presentations of the life of Jesus.

    When working with the narratives of the life of Jesus, two main types of approach have been explored thoroughly and productively by many writers over the millennia since his life. We are all familiar with these two types of approach and great benefit has been derived from these efforts. The first and most common type I call the "critical/exegetical" approach. A critical approach would search for the inconsistencies between the Gospels, or seek to sort out words, phrases, or episodes that are perceived as later additions to the original story. In these and other ways a critical approach seeks to break apart the pieces of the narrative, examine them, and then provide comment on the underlying documents.

In contrast, film presentations are the most obvious examples of a reconstructive approach. Many filmmakers have reconstructed the story of the life of Jesus and presented it on screen. These presentations frequently add scenes, events, and dialogue in an effort to present a complete story that will make sense to the viewer.

Sermons are often somewhat of a combination of these two approaches. While not all preachers begin with a critical eye toward breaking down the text, usually a pastor will begin with some form of studying the text that involves breaking down the narrative for analysis. And then the sermon is often a reconstruction of the story in an effort to make the meaning of the passage vividly captivating to the congregation.

But why not do neither? I came to believe it would be possible to resist the tendency to critique the story and at the same time resist constructing a story of my own understanding. In producing this blended translation I consciously intended to proceed according to a third way, neither critiquing the Gospels nor shaping the material in any way. This third approach begins with an axiom of accepting the integrity of the Gospel reports just as they are.

This does not mean I naively believed that I could escape the biases of my perspective. But rather it means I deliberately doubted my own sense of these events and resolved to place the reports given by these Gospels into the most natural sequence suggested by the events they report. I resolved to doubt my sense of conflict between the reports rather than doubt the reports themselves. I deliberately distrusted my sense of which reports are redundant and which reports are narrating separate events. I chose never to correct the reports by my research, but to believe the reports and look for ways that the research can support the accounts.

At first it was confusing to try to assimilate all of the information given by each of the Gospel writers. I worried that I would face a hopeless mass of detail and that what each writer said would only make sense in the context of his own larger narrative. Pushing my worries to the back of my mind I concentrated on identifying the actions that took place. All four witnesses agree that these 24 hours were a series of identifiable episodes. While the independent voice of each witness presents a first impression of conflicting stories, a remarkable unity emerged when I simply asked, What happened first? followed by the repeated question, what happened after that?

I did not begin with a set of rules governing how I would translate each segment, how I would handle redundancies, how I would form the sequence of events, etc. But in the process of simply reading the parallel passages in the original Greek text I developed consistent methods that shaped the final product.

What an experience to immerse myself in the episodes that make up the last 24 hours of the life of Jesus.

I simply went through the Greek text of the accounts of Matthew, Mark, Luke, and John, and spliced their actual words together into one unified narrative. Wherever there was complete overlap of an episode I chose the words of the

## Scenes From The Last Journey

Gospel writer who provided the greatest detail. I blended portions of one or more Gospels into the descriptions of others wherever it was necessary to complete the picture.

It is important to note that I have intended to include everything reported in the Gospels relative to these 14 scenes without adding any words of my own or leaving out anything that was reported. That does mean that these 14 episodes represent everything reported during those 24 hours. In order to construct this spiritual practice for Good Friday reading I selected the most significant events from that day in order to keep the readings from getting too long. This meditational guide presents a way of walking with Jesus through the valley of Good Friday. In this way I am presenting a personal point of view on these events because I have selected the scenes that were most important to me. It was my intention to include the main events of the story in a length that could be reasonably read on Good Friday as a means of spiritual growth.

Throughout the process of creating a blended translation, I always followed the axiom, *When in doubt, believe each writer.* In my experience, when four people have witnessed intense events and they are all telling the same story, they all have different observations to add. They all want you to know what it was like from their perspective. If they are in the same room they have a hard time keeping quiet while another is speaking. The gospel writers appear not to have read each other's accounts. So when they were writing, of course, they were not all in the same room together. But by carefully laying their accounts side by side we can hear each report in the context of the others.

My aim in the style of translation was to render each section quite literally, and yet in a way that is highly understandable to the contemporary reader of English. The style I chose is on the less-formal end of the spectrum. That choice reflects my bias toward presenting the scriptures in language that is highly accessible to everyday people.

I should note that I followed the lead of Dr. David H. Stern, translator of the *Complete Jewish Bible*, in rendering the name "Judeans" where other translations read "Jews." For a multitude of reasons I judged the term "Judean" to be a more accurate equivalent in current English usage than the word "Jew," which carries a multitude of meanings incompatible with first century realities.

A more thorough description of my process and method in making this blended translation is included in my book, *Down The Last Road: The Last Day Of The Earthly Life Of Jesus*

My blended translation of these passages is in no way meant to replace the reading of the actual standard translations of the Bible. I simply put the accounts together in this form as a way of helping you live through the last day on earth of the life of Jesus in your mind and in your heart. If my narrative strikes you as odd, or out of place, or inaccurate to what you believe happened, then I urge you to get out your own Bible and read the sections in question.

# Appendix 2

# *The Traditional 14 Stations Of The Cross*

The traditional practice of walking through the 14 stations of the cross is a wonderful idea. The practice seems to have grown naturally as people remembered Jesus every year on the day of his crucifixion. I imagine the earliest followers of Jesus visiting the locations of his suffering and remembering specific events in the very locations in which they occurred. Over the years a traditional set of places and events were established.

A certain amount of freedom is practiced in the events remembered in the stations. *The Book of Occasional Services, 2003* of the Episcopal Church describes the number and makeup of the stations this way:

The number of stations, which at first varied widely, finally became fixed at fourteen. Of these, eight are based directly on events recorded in the Gospels. The remaining six (numbers 3, 4, 6, 7, 9, and 13) are based on inferences from the Gospel account or from pious legend. If desired, these six stations may be omitted.[4]

My version of this practice is somewhat different from the traditional set of stations. I have altered the series of meditational points in three significant ways. My alteration of the list of stations should not be seen as a critique of this very important historic practice, but rather, in full appreciation the great value of this practice, I have re-shaped the Good Friday path according to a set of pastoral concerns. Anyone who uses this tool may want to know how it fits in with the church's traditional set of stations. I have reshaped the stations in the following three ways:

I have taken out the episodes that are not based on the reports of the four Gospels and replaced them with other events. I am committed to centering practices on the actual text of scripture and some of the stations in the traditional practice are based on stories from outside of the Bible. I kept the number of stations at 14 because I believe there is ancient wisdom in the format that has been practiced for many years.

My approach also differs in that the events commemorated in this book begin earlier in the journey toward the cross compared with the events in the traditional stations. The traditional stations of the cross trace the journey of Jesus

---

[4] The Book of Occasional Services, 2003, 56.

during the daylight hours on Good Friday, from when Pilate condemned him to death until his body was laid in the tomb. This traditional set of events is "walkable" in Jerusalem to this day. The distance is reasonable and the path is well-known. But since we who live in other locations are not limited by the contours and obstacles of Jerusalem, some possibilities open up for us. I took the story all of the way back to that moment at the table when Jesus predicted the betrayal. This is the moment when the shadow fell over everything. This moment emphasizes that Jesus was aware of what he faced. He knew he would be alone. And yet he embraced what was to come out of his great love. All four Gospel writers highlight that moment at the table when Jesus predicts the betrayal. And yet they also share a sense of the ignorance of the disciples in that moment. In retrospect it is clear that once Judas left the circle in order to sell Jesus out, events would go careening toward a disastrous conclusion. But in the moment the disciples were all baffled by what was happening. So my set of 14 stations begins at this moment that is a crucial turning point toward the cross.

And finally, my set of events differs from the traditional 14 stations in that I have included some events where Jesus was not present. Jesus is the center of each of the 14 traditional stations, and in that way the tradition is more pure than the guide I am presenting. I have included these other narratives in the belief that we need to place ourselves among the betrayers, the deniers, and the crucifiers in order fully comprehend the depths of forgiveness offered to us by Jesus.

My free use of the tradition is perhaps best explained by a quote from D. Elton Trueblood's book, *The Essence of Spiritual Religion*.

God does not dwell in temples made with hands, and the sense of the reality of God's presence is not dependent on any special act or group of acts. The person who experiences spiritual religion may know God in music or in silence, with spoken or unspoken prayers, with the Eucharist or without it, and, on the other hand, a person may have all the outward helps in the world without once having a vivid sense of God's real presence. Thus we may say that no particular outward aid is indispensable and that likewise no particular outward aid is sufficient in and of itself.

The understanding of the truth just stated is highly important in spiritual religion, but it must be carefully guarded or it will say too much. The fact that no *particular* outward aid is necessary does not meant that *no* outward aid is necessary. Indeed, so long as we have bodies, we cannot be free from physical stimuli and we can never escape from *some* physical media for spiritual experiences.[5]

These thoughts have been foundational to me as I have worked to develop this resource.

The following is a list of the traditional *Stations Of The Cross*.

---

[5] Trueblood, *The Essence of Spiritual Religion*, 85-86.

# The 14 Stations of the Cross

| 14 STATIONS–TRADITIONAL | 14 STATIONS IN THIS BOOK |
|---|---|
| 1. Jesus Is Condemned To Death | 1. Jesus Predicts The Betrayal |
| 2. Jesus Takes Up His Cross | 2. Prayer In The Garden |
| 3. Jesus Falls For The First Time | 3. The Arrest |
| 4. Jesus Meets His Mother | 4. Trials |
| 5. Simon Of Cyrene Helps Jesus Carry The Cross | 5. Peter Denies Knowing Jesus |
| 6. Veronica Wipes The Face Of Jesus | 6. Jesus Is Scourged And Crowned With Thorns |
| 7. Jesus Falls For The Second Time | 7. Pilate Washes His Hands Jesus Is Condemned To Death |
| 8. Jesus Meets The Women Of Jerusalem | 8. The Road To Crucifixion |
| 9. Jesus Falls For The Third Time | 9. The Soldiers Crucify Jesus |
| 10. Jesus Is Stripped Of His Garments | 10. Jesus Speaks From The Cross |
| 11. Jesus Is Nailed To The Cross | 11. Jesus Cries Out |
| 12. Jesus Dies On The Cross | 12. The Last Breath |
| 13. Jesus Is Taken Down From The Cross | 13. Jesus Is Taken Down From The Cross |
| 14. Jesus Is Laid In The Tomb | 14. Jesus Is Laid In A Tomb |

The traditional set of events has a profoundly simple focus. These scenes have given rise to some great works of art over the centuries as artists have been inspired to sculpt or paint in response to the emotion in each of these scenes.

As can be seen by making a close comparison, the first six stations in my set all take place before the beginning of the traditional set of stations. Stations 2 through 9 of the traditional set occur during the period covered by station 8, *The Road To Crucifixion,* in my set. And the last several stations are very similar in both sets.

A comparison of events may be seen more clearly when the timeline of the day is superimposed on the list of things that took place. The chart on the next page shows how the events of the traditional 14 stations compare with the stations presented in this book.

| 14 STATIONS–TRADITIONAL | 14 STATIONS IN THIS BOOK |
|---|---|
| | 1. Jesus Predicts The Betrayal |
| | 2. Prayer In The Garden |
| | 3. The Arrest |
| | 4. Trials |
| | 5. Peter Denies Knowing Jesus |

*Dawn on the morning of Good Friday*

1. Jesus Is Condemned To Death
2. Jesus Takes Up His Cross
3. Jesus Falls For The First Time
4. Jesus Meets His Mother
5. Simon Of Cyrene Helps Jesus Carry The Cross
6. Veronica Wipes The Face Of Jesus
7. Jesus Falls For The Second Time
8. Jesus Meets The Women Of Jerusalem
9. Jesus Falls For The Third Time

6. Jesus Is Scourged And Crowned With Thorns
7. Pilate Washes His Hands Jesus Is Condemned To Death

*Stations 2 through 9 Of The Traditional Set Take Place On The Road To The Place of Execution.*

8. The Road To Crucifixion

| 14 Stations–Traditional (Continued) | 14 Stations In This Book (Continued) |
|---|---|
| | 9. The Soldiers Crucify Jesus |
| 10. Jesus Is Stripped Of His Garments | 10. Jesus Speaks From The Cross |
| 11. Jesus Is Nailed To The Cross | 11. Jesus Cries Out |
| 12. Jesus Dies On The Cross | 12. The Last Breath |
| 13. Jesus Is Taken Down From The Cross | 13. Jesus Is Taken Down From The Cross |
| 14. Jesus Is Laid In The Tomb | 14. Jesus Is Laid In A Tomb |

It is my hope that my presentation of the events of this day might lend assistance in the quest to walk with Jesus through the valley of his last day on earth.

# *In Gratitude*

---

Fear is one of the bigger challenges along the way in completing a project like this. The story is so important; translating scripture is so challenging; selecting episodes out of the whole narrative is so bold; I frequently wrestled with the feeling that I should just quit. I am grateful to my friends who have helped me over the years to believe that I could do something as challenging as this. Even friends who had no direct involvement in this particular book have been entirely essential to its completion. Each one lives in my mind and heart as an encouraging presence when doubt creeps in. I am grateful to Steve Waltar, Scott Dudley, and Brian Craker among many others.

I am also grateful to my many teachers and professors of various languages over the years. I especially think of Father Elias Mallon, who patiently guided me through three years of Hebrew at the University of Washington. Insights into the way language develops, gained in the study of the historical development of Hebrew, inspired me to see dynamics in the Greek text of the New Testament.

Many translations of the scriptures are listed in the *Bibliography* section. My translation was made in consultation with those translations without any instances of copying their work. In a very few instances, *The Complete Jewish Bible*, by David H. Stern, contained some unique and insightful renderings of particular words in English. My translation reflects my agreement with him, that these are the most accurate English representations of the underlying Greek text.

Thanks to Hailey Zimmerman for interior book design and for helpful suggestions to improve an earlier version of the manuscript.

I especially want to thank:

*Annie Zimmerman*

For continuing to persevere with me as *Down The Last Road* turned into four books, thank you for your patience and encouragement.

*The Churches That Have Nurtured Me*

I am grateful to all of the churches that have walked with me along the way. Since the story of the last 24 hours of the life of Jesus is the second most important story that anyone who is part of a church must know, I feel my capacity to tell it again must be partly due to their faithfulness.

Among all of the churches I am especially grateful to–

–West Side Church in Richland, Washington, for telling me this story throughout my years of growing up.

–Tualatin Plains Presbyterian Church in Hillsboro, Oregon, for allowing me to develop the "Stations of the Cross" path as part of Good Friday observance.

–Gateway Presbyterian Church, in The Dalles, Oregon, and Cedar Creek Church, in Sherwood, Oregon, for allowing me to further develop the Good Friday story when I was part of your pastoral leadership teams.

# *Bibliography*

Aharoni, Yohanan, and Michael Avi-Yonah. *The MacMillan Bible Atlas*. New York: MacMillan Publishing, 1977.

Aland, Kurt, Ed. *Synopsis Of The Four Gospels,* Seventh Edition. Stuttgart, Germany: German Bible Society, 1984.

Aland, Kurt, Matthew Black, Carlo M. Martin, Bruce M. Metzger, and Allen Wikgren, eds. *The Greek New Testament*, 3rd. Edition (corrected). Stuttgart, Germany: United Bible Societies, 1983.

Bagster, Samuel & Sons. *The Analytical Greek Lexicon*. New York: Harper & Brothers, 1959.

Calvin, John. *Commentary On A Harmony Of The Evangelists, Matthew, Mark, And Luke*. Tr. William Pringle. Grand Rapids, Michigan: Baker Book House, 1996.

———. *Commentary On The Gospel Of John*. Volume One. Tr. William Pringle. Grand Rapids, Michigan: Baker Book House, 1996.

Cheney, Johnston M., and Stanley Ellisen. *Jesus Christ The Greatest Life: A Unique Blending Of The Four Gospels*. Eugene, Oregon: Paradise, 1999.

Chrysostom, John. *Homilies Of St. John Chrysostom On The Gospel According To St. John*. Translated and Edited by Philip Schaff. The Nicene and Post-Nicene Fathers, First Series, v. XIV. Grand Rapids, Michigan: Eerdmans, 1956.

Church Publishing. *The Book Of Occasional Services • 2003*. New York: Church Publishing, 2004.

Cullmann, Oscar. "The Plurality of the Gospels as a Theological Problem in Antiquity." Chapter 2 in *The Early Church: Studies In Early Christian History & Theology*. Edited by A. J. B. Higgins. Abridged edition. Philadelphia: The Westminster Press, 1966.

Dana, H. E., and Julius R. Mantey. *A Manual Grammar of the Greek New Testament*. New York: MacMillan, 1927.

deSilva, David A. *An Introduction To The New Testament: Contexts, Methods & Ministry Formation*. Second Edition. Downers Grove, Illinois: IVP Academic, 2018.

Dix, Gregory. *The Shape Of The Liturgy*. Second Edition. London: Dacre Press, 1945.

Edersheim, Alfred. *The Life And Times Of Jesus The Messiah*. Grand Rapids, Michigan: Eerdmans, 1971.

Edwards, James R. *The Gospel According to Mark*. The Pillar New Testament Commentary. Grand Rapids, Michigan: William B. Eerdmans, 2002.

Elowsky, Joel C., ed. *The Ancient Christian Commentary on Scripture: New Testament, IV b, John 11-21*. Thomas C. Oden, General Editor. Downers Grove, Illinois: InterVarsity, 2007.

*Good News Bible: The Bible in Today's English Version*. New York: American Bible Society, 1976.

Han, Nathan E. *A Parsing Guide To The Greek New Testament*. Scottdale, Pennsylvania: Herald Press, 1971.

*Holy Bible, New Living Translation*. Wheaton, Illinois: Tyndale House, 1996.

*The Holy Bible, New Revised Standard Version: Containing The Old And New Testaments With The Apocryphal/Deuterocanonical Books*. New York: Oxford University Press, 1989.

Hoskyns, Edwyn Clement. *The Fourth Gospel*. 2nd ed., revised. Edited by Francis Noel Davey. London: Faber and Faber Limited, 1947.

Johnson, Luke Timothy. *Living Jesus: Learning the Heart of the Gospel*. New York: HarperSanFrancisco, a Division of Harper Collins Publishers. 1999.

Just Jr., Arthur A. *The Ancient Christian Commentary on Scripture: New Testament, III, Luke*. Thomas C. Oden, General Editor. Downers Grove, Illinois: InterVarsity, 2003.

*KJV Giant-Print Classic Reference Bible*. Grand Rapids, Michigan: Zondervan, 1994.

Kohlenberger III, John R., Edward W. Goodrick, and James A. Swanson. *The Exhaustive Concordance To The Greek New Testament*. Zondervan Greek Reference Series. Grand Rapids, Michigan: Zondervan, 1995.

The Lockman Foundation. *New American Standard Bible*. Carol Stream, Illinois: Creation House, 1973.

Major, H.D.A., T.W. Manson, and C.J. Wright. *The Mission And Message of Jesus: An Exposition Of The Gospels In The Light Of Modern Research*. New York: E. P. Dutton And Co., 1938.

Marshall, Alfred. *The Interlinear NRSV–NIV: Parallel New Testament In Greek And English*. Grand Rapids, Michigan: Zondervan Publishing House, 1993.

Marshall, I. Howard. *Commentary on Luke*. New International Greek Testament Commentary. Grand Rapids, Michigan: William B. Eerdmans Publishing Company, 1978.

———. *Last Supper And Lord's Supper*. Carlisle, U.K.: Paternoster, 1980.

Metzger, Bruce M. *A Textual Commentary On The Greek New Testament.* New York: United Bible Societies, 1971.

Morris, Leon. *The Gospel According To John.* The New International Commentary On The New Testament. Grand Rapids, Michigan: Wm. B. Eerdmans, 1971.

Nestle, Eberhard, and Nestle, Erwin. *Novum Testamentum Graece.* 17th edition. Stuttgart: Privileg. Württ. Bibelanstalt, 1953.

Oden, Thomas C.., and Christopher A. Hall, eds. *The Ancient Christian Commentary on Scripture: New Testament, II, Mark.* Thomas C. Oden, General Editor. Downers Grove, Illinois: InterVarsity, 1998.

Ogilvie, Lloyd John. *The Cup of Wonder: Communion Meditations.* Wheaton, Illinois: Tyndale House, 1976.

Plummer, Alfred. *An Exegetical Commentary On The Gospel According To St. Matthew.* Grand Rapids, Michigan: Eerdmans, 1953.

Rat der Evangelischen Kirche in Deutschland. *Die Bibel oder die ganze Heilige Schrifte des Alten und Neuen Testaments.* Vienna, Austria: Österreichische Bibelgesellschaft, 1976.

Robertson, A.T. *A Grammar Of The Greek New Testament In The Light Of Historical Research.* Nashville, Tennessee: Broadman, 1934.

Simonetti, Manlio, ed. *The Ancient Christian Commentary on Scripture: New Testament, Ib, Matthew 14-28*. Thomas C. Oden, General Editor. Downers Grove, Illinois: InterVarsity, 2002.

Stern, David H. *Complete Jewish Bible*. Clarksville, Maryland: Jewish New Testament Publications, 1998.

Strong, James. *Strong's Exhaustive Concordance Of The Bible*. Nashville, Tennessee: Thomas Nelson.

The Trinitarian Bible Society. *The New Testament: The Greek Text Underlying The English Authorised Version of 1611*. London: The Trinitarian Bible Society, 1976.

Trueblood, D. Elton. *The Essence Of Spiritual Religion*. New York: Harper &Row, 1975.

Wilson, Neil S., and Linda K. Taylor. *Tyndale Handbook Of Bible Charts and Maps*. Carol Stream, Illinois: Tyndale House, 2001.

Zerwick, Max S.J. *A Grammatical Analysis Of The Greek New Testament*. Translated by Mary Grosvenor. Unabridged 3rd. Rev. Ed. Rome: Editrice Pontificio Istituto Biblico, 1988.

# The *Down The Last Road* series

What started as a single blended translation has grown into four publications designed to make the story easy to use for individuals, for families, and for churches. This series of resources has been developed in order to present this story in the best possible ways for different audiences. Consider how you might use these to present this narrative in ways that will serve various needs.

Whether sitting quietly alone, simply reading the simple story, or encountering narrative in other creative ways, you can make this day in the life of Jesus a life-changing part of how you see the world. Four different publications are available to make the meaning of this story more vivid in your experience.

# Down The Last Road
## The Last Day of the Earthly Life of Jesus

This blended narrative presents a complete account of everything the Gospels report concerning the last day of the earthly life of Jesus. Included in this volume you will find a simple, meditational version of the narrative, along with *Study Notes* with all of the scripture references included in detail.

This book presents the basic form of the narrative that is used for each of these resources.

# Scenes From The Last Journey
## 14 Points On The Way of the Cross

The 14 events recounted in this book come directly from the pages of the four gospels. So these are not identical with the traditional 14 stations, but rather our 14 stations have been designed to reflect the Biblical accounts from the betrayal and arrest until Jesus is laid in the tomb.

*Coming In 2022*

# The Last Day

A Play In Two Acts

This script contains the complete narrative of that last day, from just before the last supper up to the moment when the remaining friends of Jesus walked away from his tomb. The script was created straight from the text of the blended translation contained in *Down The Last Road*. All quotations were simply converted into spoken parts for the characters in the play. A narrator's part utilizes the precise words from the Gospels to set the scene for the dialogue that takes place.

The play is designed to be presented as a Readers Theater performance, so no costumes, sets, or line memorization is required.

Separated into two Acts, the play may either be presented all at once, or in two separate performances. Act 1 covers the events of Maundy Thursday, from the Upper Room to the arrest in the garden. Act 2 moves to the trial, abuse, and crucifixion. With a little planning you will be able to perform either a two Act play on Maundy Thursday, or put on twoseparate performances on Maundy Thursday and Good Friday.

For the sake of facilitating performance, the script will be available in two forms.

# The Last Day

## Director's Script

With extensive instructions, suggestions and notes, the Director's version of the script covers everything a director will want to know to lead a group of readers to perform the play. This will guide your preparations and help you know how many copies of the Reader's Script will be needed.

# The Last Day

## Reader's Script

This contains the simple script in two acts. To perform the reading, order enough copies to give one to each participant. The number of participants may vary based on how you choose to divide the readings. Guidance for this is found in the Director's Script, and it will be helpful to read that guidance before determining the number of Reader's Scripts to order for your performance.

*Look for these scripts to be available in time for Holy Week of 2022.*

# ABOUT THE AUTHOR

Richard P. Zimmerman is a pastor and writer who has served in several congregations in the Pacific Northwest and Alaska. He holds degrees from the University of Washington (B.A.), Princeton Theological Seminary (M. Div.), Regent College in Vancouver, B.C. (Th. M.), and Columbia Theological Seminary (D. Min.). He also completed a year of advanced study in Northwest Semitic Languages at the University of Chicago.

Having a special interest in the languages of the Bible world has led him to take extensive courses in Greek, Hebrew, and related languages.

Richard makes his home the Pacific Northwest with his wife, Annie. They enjoy hiking, skiing and snowboarding, golf, and just generally being outside in God's creation.

ALSO BY RICHARD P. ZIMMERMAN

*Walk With Me To Another Land: A Narrative Approach to Transitional Ministry*

*Launch: A Guide For The Season of Lent*

www.ingramcontent.com/pod-product-compliance
Lightning Source LLC
Chambersburg PA
CBHW051404290426
44108CB00015B/2144